CAN YOU MAKE A FRYING PAN OUT OF PAPER?

by Michelle Hilderbrand

PEBBLE

a capstone imprint

Published by Pebble, an imprint of Capstone
1710 Roe Crest Drive, North Mankato, Minnesota 56003
capstonepub.com

Library of Congress Cataloging-in-Publication Data is available
on the Library of Congress website
ISBN: 9781666350890 (hardcover)
ISBN: 9781666350951 (paperback)
ISBN: 9781666351019 (ebook PDF)

Summary: Paper has lots of different properties and is used in lots
of items. Learn more about different types of paper, their many uses,
and if you could really use paper to make a frying pan.

Editorial Credits
Editor: Christianne Jones; Designer: Elyse White; Media Researcher:
Morgan Walters; Production Specialist: Polly Fisher

Image Credits
Getty Images: Alexander Sorokopud, 13, simarik, 16; Shutterstock:
Andrenko Tatiana, right Cover, Anke van Wyk, 14, Chaikom, middle
7, Dudareva1386, 9, goldenporshe, 10, Mangkorn Danggura, 19,
melnikof, 11, Monkey Business Images, 5, Oxie99, middle left 7,
Pasuwan, 20, phloxii, 17, Roschetzky Photography, 15, sabyna75,
middle right 7, Sergey Skleznev, left Cover, Tyler Olson, 6

All internet sites appearing in back matter were available and
accurate when this book was sent to press.

Printed and bound in the USA. PO4882

Table of Contents

Words in **bold** are in the glossary.

A Paper Frying Pan?

Frying pans are made of metal. The metal of the pan needs heat to cook food. Metal that frying pans are made of must be light enough to carry. The metal needs to be solid and **reusable**.

Do you think you could make a frying pan out of paper? Let's find out!

Properties of Paper

Paper is a thin material. It is light. There are many kinds of paper. Some paper is used to make books. Other kinds of paper are used to make boxes and packaging.

Paper being sewn together to make a book

wood pulp

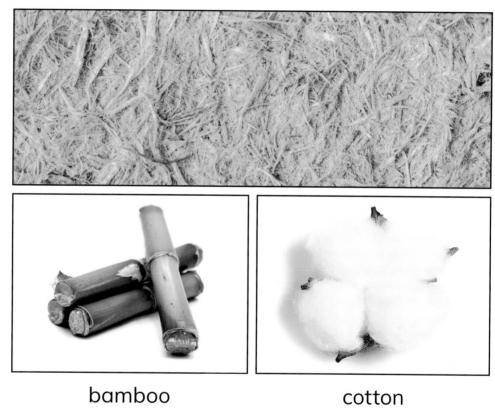

bamboo   cotton

Paper is mostly made from wood **pulp** or
other natural **fibers** like bamboo or cotton.

Making Paper

Papermaking started in China hundreds of years ago. It used to be done by hand. But what did people write on before they had paper?

They would write on anything they could find! They wrote on cloth. They wrote on stone walls. They wrote on wood. Paper made things a lot easier!

Before paper was invented,
Egyptian people wrote on walls.

Now paper is made by machines. Paper is made by pressing wet natural fibers onto a screen.

Then they are rolled out. A machine presses all the water out. Then the fibers are left to dry. Once dried, these fibers become paper.

Types of Paper

Paper comes in different types for different uses. Sometimes paper is coated with **chemicals**. They change the **texture** of the paper.

Smooth paper is better for printing. Textured paper is better for drawing.

The weight of paper matters too. Thin
paper is light and easy to tear, like a letter
you get in the mail.

Thick and heavy paper is strong. It doesn't bend easily. Packages that come in the mail are usually made from thicker paper or cardboard.

Using Paper

Paper is used to make books, money, toilet paper, magazines, and egg cartons. Fun items like confetti are made from paper too!

The most common uses of paper are for printing, packaging, writing, and making cardboard. Can you think of other items made from paper?

Paper and Frying Pans

You could make paper into the shape of a frying pan. The paper would be strong enough to hold the shape of a pan. But it would fall apart if it got wet.

Paper burns easily. That wouldn't be very good for cooking.

Could you make a frying pan out of paper? Would you?

Paper Plane

Paper is used for so many things. You can even use it to make a toy!

What You Need:

- a few pieces of paper

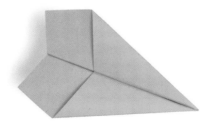

What You Do:

1. Set one piece of paper on a table.

2. Fold your paper in half the long way, then unfold.

3. Fold the upper corners into the center of paper.

4. Fold in half the long way again.

5. Fold the top half down to the bottom half on both sides.

6. Now let your plane fly!

Glossary

chemical (KE-muh-kuhl)—a substance used in or produced by chemistry; medicines, gunpowder, and food preservatives all are made from chemicals

fiber (FI-bur)—a long, thin thread of material, such as cotton, wool, or silk

pulp (PULP)—broken down fibers that are used to make other things

reusable (ree-yoo-zuh-BUHL)—able to be used again

texture (TEKS-chur)—the way something feels

Read More

Howes, Katey. *Be a Maker*. Minneapolis: Carolrhoda Books, 2019.

Meister, Cari. *From Trees to Paper*. Mankato, MN: Amicus Ink, 2020.

Rivera, Andrea. *Paper*. Minneapolis: Abdo Zoom, 2018.

Internet Sites

Britannica Kids: Paper
kids.britannica.com/kids/article/paper/399561

DK Findout!: Chinese Paper-making
dkfindout.com/us/history/ancient-china/chinese-paper-making

Kiddle: Paper Facts for Kids
kids.kiddle.co/Paper

Index

About the Author

Michelle Hilderbrand is a writer and editor in Southwest Minnesota. She enjoys skating and reading books in her free time.